CONTENTS

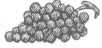

Harvesting after Petrus De Crescentiis woodcut from the 'Liber Ruralium Commodorum' first published in 1471

THE LITTLE
RED WINE

BOOK

Judy Ridgway

GUILD PUBLISHING
LONDON · NEW YORK · SYDNEY · TORONTO

© 1989 Judy Piatkus (Publishers) Limited

This edition published 1989 by
Guild Publishing by arrangement with
Judy Piatkus (Publishers) Ltd

CN 2406

Drawings by Trevor Newton
Cover photograph by Theo Bergström

Printed and bound in Great Britain

INTRODUCTION

'Wine is the alcoholic beverage obtained from the fermentation of the juice of freshly gathered grapes, the fermentation taking place in the district of origin according to local tradition and practice.'

This is the EEC definition of wine and it includes all the essential elements which go into making wine. 'Wines' from fruit other than grapes are not included in the definition.

Surprisingly, the exact nature of fermentation was not fully understood until about a century ago and wine-making could be a very chancy business. Modern technology has meant that much of the guesswork has been taken out of cultivating vines and making wine, but fine wines still depend on considerable care and skill from both grower and maker.

HISTORY OF WINE

Bacchanalian Revel
after Nicolas Poussin

Wine-making originated in ancient Persia. Vines were cultivated on the southern slopes of the Caucasus Mountains, flanked by the Caspian and the Black Sea. From Persia the craft spread in all directions, but the Babylonians became particularly keen wine-makers. There is even a wine list dating from the time of King Nebuchadnezzar in existence today.

As travellers traversed the shores of the Mediterranean, so the wine-making skills spread. Soon the Greeks and the Romans had the vine and both of them rated the commodity it produced so highly that, each in turn, they dedicated a god to wine. The Greek Dionysus and the Roman Bacchus were both high-ranking dieties.

The Romans carried on the spread of the vine by taking it inland up the river valleys and away from the sea. They developed frost-proof vines and planted them in Bordeaux and along the valleys of the Rhône, Marne, Seine, Mosel and Rhine, and vines even found their way as far east as Hungary and as far west and north as York, England.

The Romans were converted to Christianity, and as their empire collapsed and the legions returned to Italy and the East, the early Christian missionaries and monks carried on the skills of viticulture and wine-making. They needed sacramental wines and so wherever they built a church, they planted a vineyard.

The Dark Ages saw little progress in wine production. Some wine came to England via the Netherlands, and in Spain the Moors, rather surprisingly in view of their Muslim faith, improved the culture of the vine there.

The Norman conquest of England coincided with an upsurge in demand for wine all across Europe and the export of wine became an important part of contemporary trading. The marriage of Eleanor of Aquitaine to King Henry II of England opened the way for the Bordeaux wine/English wool trade. Wines from Gascony, Poitou, Burgundy and Languedoc were also shipped in vast quantities and some of it found its way on to other parts of northern Europe. Wine certainly reached Scotland where Alexander III was so keen on it that he ran up a bill of £2,000, no mean sum in those days, to one Gascony merchant.

Wine from the Bordeaux region came to be known in England as claret and that name has stuck ever since.* There was an attempt recently by the EEC to enforce the use of the term 'red Bordeaux' instead. However, it was pointed out that the English crown had owned the Bordeaux region for nearly 300 years and that even after being obliged to quit their holding, the English had continued to buy very large quantities of Bordeaux wine. The EEC gave in.

In 1353, alliances within Europe were changing and the British signed the Treaty of Windsor with Portugal, thus establishing the beginning of the port wine trade. That, too, has continued to this day, though trade is not on quite the same scale as it used to be. In the eighteenth century port wine was relatively cheap compared with French wine, and the Methuen Treaty of 1703 gave Portuguese wine preferential rates of duties. As a result, many English wine-merchants made their headquarters in Oporto and became so important that they set up their own courts of law there. Many of their descendants remain there still.

Over the years, the taxes levied generally on wine imports grew and by the early nineteenth century wine was far too expensive a drink for any but those living in a wine-growing area, or the wealthy, to enjoy. Gin and beer were the tipples of the growing industrial towns.

* The story has it that the red wines of Bordeaux were lighter in colour – *plus clair* – than those which came from further inland, hence claret.

The twentieth century has seen a number of changes in the pattern of the wine trade. Exports of port and sherry to the UK, once the major outlet for these drinks, started to fall and in the USA Prohibition meant that nothing but illegal hooch was sold.

However, the last twenty years have seen the emergence of a major challenge to the traditional wine-producing areas of Europe. This has been the development of a flourishing wine-making business, first in California and more recently in Australia. This has meant that those areas and countries which do not grow their own wine now have a much greater choice on the off-licence or supermarket shelves than ever before.

'Frenchmen drink wine just like we used to drink water before Prohibition.'

Wits End (1973)
R.E. Drennan

GROWING VINES

Vines need plenty of sunshine in summer to ripen the grapes. They also need a cool enough winter to enable them to rest and gather strength for the coming growing season. In the northern hemisphere the northern limit is set around latitude 50°, the southern limit at 30°. In the southern hemisphere the latitudes are reversed. Within these 'wine' belts vines will grow well, but some varieties will tolerate the lack of sun or excess heat at the edges rather better than others.

In England, for example, there is only sufficient sun to fully ripen a grape crop in the open two years out of five; and it is not possible to guarantee a frost-free period when the flowers are forming. This means that English growers cannot easily grow red grape varieties, which generally need more sun to ripen than white ones.

The overall climate of an area is a critical factor in the choice of grapes to grow and this applies not only to large areas of the world, but also from country to country and from district to district. Thus the Atlantic climate of Bordeaux suits the Cabernet Sauvignon grape, whereas the hot valley of the Rhône is better suited to the more robust Syrah.

The soil also plays an important part, but there is a saying that the best wines come from the poorest soils. The vine seems to flourish where other crops will not. The vine does not need nitrogen as much as other plants, but what it does need is plenty of mineral elements in the soil. These are essential to the delicate flavours of different wines. Volcanic soils, limestone, chalk and granite all produce different wines.

The microclimate and the soil of a small area or even a single vineyard can affect the qualities of the finished wine to such an extent that an expert wine-taster will be able to identify exactly where the grapes used to make the wine were grown.

GRAFTING

Nowadays most vines are grated on to American root stocks. This is to protect them from a root-eating plant louse called Phylloxera, which almost completely destroyed European vineyards in the late nineteenth century. The louse came to Europe from America and the American vines were found to be resistant. The only problem was that these American grapes give a very distinctive 'foxy' taste to wine, which is not much liked. The answer which the farmers finally came up with was to graft European vines on to American root stocks and, except in a few isolated places, that is the way vines are now grown throughout the world.

THE VINEYARD YEAR

In the northern hemisphere, the vineyard year starts after the vintage in late October or early November when the vineyards are generally tidied. The land is ploughed and soil is built up around the roots to protect the vine during the winter. December and January involve general maintenance.

February is the main pruning season and cuttings are taken from grafts. Pruning is finished in March, the roots are cleared of soil and grafting starts. In April the shoots begin to grow and are fastened to the wires or trellises in the vineyards. This is followed by the first spraying in May and flowering and pollination in June. Planting of new sections of the vineyard take place in May.

Spraying will continue as necessary through the summer and in July the grapes will be clearly visible. There may be a summer pruning now to allow more light and sunshine to the fruit and to stop the leaves taking over. The grapes begin to swell and change colour and the wine-making equipment is prepared. In September the grapes are nearing maturity and they are tested for sugar. The harvest generally runs from mid-September to mid-October.

WORLD PRODUCTION

Italy and France lead the world in wine production. Trailing well behind in third place is Spain, with the USSR and Argentina in fourth and fifth places.

GRAPES AND GRAPE VARIETIES

Wine is made from a specific type of grape called *Vitis vinifera*. These grapes are used only for making wine. They are not table grapes and would probably taste very bitter if you tried to eat them.

Grapes are made up of a thick skin which contains colour and a central pulp which has no colour at all. If you removed the skins from red grape varieties and used them to make wine, the wine would be white.

The skin also contains tannins and so for red wine it is important to ferment the grapes with their skins. The pulp contains sugar, fruit acids, water and pectins, all of which are important in wine-making. The pips contain bitter oils which are not wanted.

On the outside of the grapes is a whitish bloom. This waxy substance traps three organisms which are important in wine making. These are wild yeasts, wine yeasts and bacteria. The wild yeasts and the bacteria are not wanted in the wine-making process, but they need air to live and so can be excluded by being deprived of air. Luckily the wine yeasts, which are wanted, are able to work in the absence of oxygen.

There are many different varieties of *Vitis vinifera*. Originally, each one grew in a particular part of Europe. However, some grape varieties such as Cabernet Sauvignon and Pinot Noir were considered to produce better wine than some of the others, and so their use spread to others parts of Europe and more recently to the New World.

The best grape varieties for producing fine wine are known as classic varieties.

CLASSIC GRAPES

CABERNET SAUVIGNON Cabernet Sauvignon is probably one of the most widely grown grapes in the world. It is the red grape variety of Bordeaux and is the basis for most claret. It is also grown on a smaller scale in the Loire Valley and in Provence.

Outside France it crops up in large quantities in Australia and in California. In the former country it may be used on its own or be mixed with the Australian Shiraz grape. In California it usually comes as a 'varietal' wine unmixed with other grapes. Chile, South Africa and Bulgaria are also quite large producers, and experimental wines are selling well from Spain and Italy.

The Cabernet Sauvignon grape produces wine with a characteristic blackcurrant aroma and flavour. The wines are suitable for long ageing, though those from the New World are often so fruity and opulent that they are drunk quite young. The Cabernet Sauvignon also has plenty of tannin which is important in wines for laying down and keeping.

MERLOT   Originating from Bordeaux, the Merlot produces a soft and quite fruity wine which is blended with Cabernet Franc and Cabernet Sauvignon. It is also grown extensively in Bergerac and is starting to be grown in Languedoc-Roussillon and other parts of southwestern France. Outside of France it is grown in northeastern Italy and, in a small way, in California.

PINOT NOIR   This grape is also from a classic French wine-growing area, this time from Burgundy. Unlike Cabernet Sauvignon, the Pinot Noir does not transplant very well, and though vignerons do try to grow it in the US and in Australia, the end results do not have the intensity of Burgundian wine.

Pinot Noir is also grown in other parts of France – in the Loire as red Sancerre and in Alsace – as well as in Germany and northern Italy. The resulting wines are quite pale in colour, often quite acidic, and much lighter than the classic from Burgundy.

At its best, Pinot Noir has a wonderfully sweet, ripe strawberry aroma and flavour which mellows to a complex fruity but vegetal taste. It ages well, though not perhaps for quite as long as wines made from Cabernet Sauvignon.

SYRAH This is *the* grape of the northern Rhône Valley in France and is used in great wines such as Côte Rôtie and Hermitage. It is not grown much elsewhere, except in Australia. There it is known as the Shiraz and has traditionally not been considered of great merit, though it is the base of the famous Grande Hermitage. Today this attitude is beginning to change and the variety is increasingly being mixed with Cabernet Sauvignon to produce some first-class wines.

Syrah produces deeply coloured tannic wines which are very full-bodied. The best wines may take years to reach full maturity and so they age well.

'Let's have Wine and Women, mirth and laughter
Sermons and soda water the day after.'

Don Juan, Lord Byron (1788–1824)

NON-CLASSIC GRAPES

CABERNET FRANCE: Used in the classic claret blend and has a light blackcurranty aroma and flavour. It is also grown in the Loire for Saumur, Touraine, Chinon and Burgeuil wines.

GAMAY: Used in making Beaujolais wines. This grape has an uncomplicated jammy flavour.

GRENACHE: Used in the Châteauneuf-du-Pape blend and in plenty of southern Rhône wines. This is also the Garnacha used in many Spanish wines.

NEBBIOLO: Used in making Barolo from Piemonte. This grape makes a very tannic wine which takes years to mature.

SANGROVES: Used in making Chianti, this grape is particularly acidic. At its best, it also has good fruit and tannin content.

TEMPRANILLO: Used in making Rioja, this grape has a deeply coloured skin which gives a rich colour to the wine.

'Drink wine and have the gout; drink no wine and have the gout too.'

Proverb

How Red Wine Is Made

Wine-making depends on the enzyme action of wine yeasts converting the sugar from the grapes into alcohol. The process is known as fermentation, during which gas and heat are given off as well as alcohol.

When the grapes first reach the winery they are lightly crushed so that their skins break, bringing the yeasts into contact with the sugar in the pulp. The grapes and their skins are called the must, and this is fed into huge fermentation vats. Sulphur dioxide is added to take up the oxygen in the must and to form a blanket over the top. This kills off the wild yeasts and bacteria which cannot live in the absence of oxygen.

Quite often specially developed wine yeasts are added to the must to be sure of the right results, and fermentation starts. This is very fast and violent at first, but then things quieten down. Fermentation will continue slowly for another three to four weeks or more.

When the required amount of colour and tannin has been extracted from the skins, the liquid part of the must is run off from the bottom of the vat. The skins still contain quite a lot of liquid and so they are moved through a press where the remaining juice is recovered. The wine-maker then decides whether he will add some or all of this to the first-run liquid.

The still-fermenting wine is then put to mature in wooden casks. As fermentation slows, so the wine cools and shrinks; a certain amount also sinks into the wood, so it is necessary to top up the casks at least once a week.

During the first three months of maturation, the wine will throw a sediment consisting of dead yeasts. If left, this sediment will decompose and spoil the wine, so the wine is carefully taken off and pumped into another cask. This racking process is carried out once every three months until the wine is bottled. Prior to bottling, the wine needs to be cleared, or fined. A substance such as egg white or an absorbent earth such as kieselguhr is added, and all the bits and pieces remaining in the wine adhere to the fining agent and sink to the bottom. Some wines are also filtered before bottling.

Wine is a mixture of many things which continue to act on each other until the wine is drunk. It continues to mature in the bottle and the optimum time to consume the wine will vary from wine to wine.

'Come in, you Anglo Saxon swine
And drink my Algerian wine.
'Twill turn your eyeballs black and blue,
And damn well good enough for you.'

Painted as an advertisement on the window
of a Paris Café: *My Life with Brendan*
(referring to Brendan Behan, 1923–1964)

MAJOR RED WINE
PRODUCING REGIONS
OF THE WORLD

AMERICA

California is the most important wine-growing area in the United States of America. The same grapes are grown here as in Europe, but with the addition of Zinfandel, a red grape peculiar to the USA. The wines made from this grape can be big and beefy or light and white!

The vines are planted in the valley floors and on the lower slopes. The Napa Valley was one of the first areas to produce fine wines and many of the best-known wineries are there.

Most of the wines are produced as varietal wines from one grape variety rather than as blends. If a variety is stated on the label, the wine must contain at least 75% of that variety. The best wines tend to be fairly full-flavoured and some have great ageing potential.

Oregon and Washington State are both making great strides in producing fine wines comparable to those of California. Being further north, they are experimenting with Pinot Noir and some of the wines are very good indeed.

AUSTRALIA

In the early days of Australian wine-making, the producers simply made a wine, decided which French wine it most closely resembled and sold, for example, Australian Burgundy. Much of it was sweet and rather heavy.

With the advent of the EEC, this type of labelling was made illegal in Europe. At the same time, Australian demand for wine also started to become more sophisticated. These changes have resulted in today's range of lively red wines.

Australian red wines are now made predominently from the Cabernet Sauvignon and Syrah or Shiraz. They are very fruity and full-flavoured with a distinctive taste of their own. The best ones can hold their own with any of the great French wines.

These wines are sold either blended or as varietals. Some of the better-known areas for red wine are the Barossa Valley and Coonawarrah in South Australia, Hunter River Valley in New South Wales and Rutherglen in Victoria.

BULGARIA

The state-run wine industry in Bulgaria has developed some very good value-for-money red wines which find their way mainly to the West. They are based on the Cabinet Sauvignon grape which is grown in the north and east of the country, with more traditional, national varieties growing in the south. An area producing particularly good wine is Pleven.

CHILE

The vineyards of Chile are remarkable in that they have never been attacked by the root louse phylloxera and so all the vines grow on their own root stocks.

The original vineyards were developed by the Spaniards and some of the best wines today are made by Spanish companies. The wines for export must be described according to their age, as Courant for one year old, Special for two years old, Reserve for four years old and Gran Vino for six years old or more.

FRANCE

Bordeaux is one of the most important wine-producing areas of France. Claret is the English name given to wines from this area, and the châteaux which produce claret are among the most famous red wine names in the world. They include such names as Lafite, Latour and Mouton Rothschild in the Haut Medoc and Chateau Petrus in Pomerol.

The main grape varieties are Cabernet Sauvignon, which is predominant in the Medoc wines of the left bank of the Gironde, and Merlot which is more important in St. Emillion and Pomerol on the right bank. Cabernet Franc is also used in the various blends.

The wines range from straightforward table wines for early drinking to first-class wines which are made to last and which take many years to mature. Both the Medoc and St. Emillion have detailed classification systems based on the location of the vineyard or château. Also falling within the Bordeaux umbrella are the areas of Graves, Premières Côtes de Bordeaux, Fronsac, Côtes de Bordeaux, Fronsac, Côtes de Bourg and Premières Côtes de Blaye.

Burgundy vies with Bordeaux for the role of top wine-maker. Some enthusiasts prefer one, some the other. Unlike Bordeaux, the best wines are made from a single grape variety, the Pinot Noir, but the classification system, like that of the other wine-growing areas, depends on the location of the vineyards.

The finest wines are found in the regions of the Côte de Nuit which takes in Gevrey-Chambertin, Nuits St.-Georges and Vongeot and the Côte de Beaune, which includes Beaune itself along with Corton, Pommard and Volnay.

Further south, Mercurey and Mâcon produce quite good red wines from the Pinot Noir. At the southernmost part of Burgundy is the Beaujolais. Here Gamay grapes are grown to produce all styles of wine, from the light Nouveau styles, through Beaujolais and Beaujolais Village to the better wines of the Cru villages, such as Fleurie, Morgon and Moulin-à-Vent. In good years, these wines age well and can be kept for three or four years or more.

Loire is predominantly a white wine area, but red wine is made from Cabernet Franc, Cabernet Sauvignon and Gamay grapes, and even the Pinot Noir is grown in Sancere. Apellations include Anjou, Touraine, Saumur, Bourgueil and Chinon.

The northernpart of the *Rhône Valley* produces some really first-class red wines from the Syrah grape. These wines are full-bodied and tannic and take some years to mature. They include Côte Rôtie, Hermitage and Cornas. A slightly lighter wine is Crozes-Hermitage.

In the southern Rhône, the number of grape varieties grown blossoms out into quite a long list, including Grenache, Carignan and Cinsault among others. The most common appellation is Côtes du Rhône, but there are also Gigondas and

Châteauneuf-du-Pape. The latter may use as many as nine or more grape varieties.

Provence uses similar grape varieties to those grown in the southern Rhône with the addition of Mourvèdre. The wines vary from light drinking wines to quite serious wines with some ageing potential.

The huge area of *southwest France* produces masses of wine which often ends up in the European wine lake. However, there are some areas such as Fitou, Corbières and Cahors which are producing some very interesting and reasonable red wines.

HUNGARY

Bull's Blood is probably the best-known Hungarian wine outside of Hungary. It is made in the north of the country from a mixture of traditional grapes.

It got its name from an episode in the history of Eger, the town where the wine is made. The story goes that it was Bull's Blood that fortified the inhabitants of Eger in their battle against invading Turks. When the Turks saw the Hungarians with their beards stained red from the wine, they ran in terror, thinking that their enemies were drinking the blood of bulls!

ITALY

Tuscany produces Chianti which is probably the most popular of Italian reds. It is made predominantly from the Sangiovese grape together with a small mix of two or three other varieties. For many years, the younger wines made for immediate drinking were bottled in straw-covered bottles or *fiaschi*, but these are now fast disappearing.

All Chianti is classified as DOCG wine, the highest level of the Italian classification system, but some Chiantis do not really merit this level of classification. The best Chianti comes from the Chianti Classico region of central Tuscany. It can easily be recognised by the Gallo Nero, or black cock, symbol on every bottle.

The wines of Chianti Classico are made to last. When they are young they can be quite tannic, and like all Italian red wines they have a high level of acidity. Good examples also have plenty of fruit flavours.

Some of the best red wines of Italy are produced in Tuscany, but confusingly they do not carry any classification other than table wine. The reason is that the producers are experimenting with grape varieties which are either not included in the DOCG laws, or which may only be used in limited amounts. Here it is usually the high price rather than the label, which indicates the quality!

Piemonte is the other great wine-producing area of Italy. The Nebbiolo grape is used to produce Barolo wines. These, too, carry the classification DOCG. They are very hard tannic wines, which are aged in wooden casks for quite a long time before bottling. This sometimes means that they lose much of their fruit.

Emiglia-Romana is the region which produces the popular Lambrusco wines. These red wines are sweetish and slightly sparkling.

PORTUGAL

Fortified wines from Portugal, in the shape of port wine, have been finding their way round the world for many centuries but the lighter table wines are not so well known. However, all this is changing as Portugal takes its place in the Common Market.

Dão wines are probably the best known of the Portuguese table wines. The Dão has been a denominated region since the early part of the century. Its wines are aged for long periods in wooden casks and, like Barolo, the wine tends to lose its fruity flavours.

Other areas which are coming to the fore are the Bairrada, producing a red wine from the Baga grape which ages well, the Ribatejo and the Alentejo, both producing excellent, easy to drink wines at very reasonable prices, and the Douro which is now producing light as well as fortified wine.

SOUTH AFRICA

The vineyards in South Africa were first planted in 1652 and some of the old estates, such as Constantia, are still in production.

The most common grape varieties are Cabernet Sauvignon, Shiraz and Pinotage. The latter is a cross between Pinot Noir and Hermitage or Cinsault. Fortified wines of the port type are produced as well as light table wines.

SPAIN

Rioja is the best-known red wine producing area of Spain. The wines are full-bodied, well-flavoured and usually very long-lasting. They are made only from traditional grape varieties, but are sometimes likened to those of Burgundy.

Considerable importance is attached to ageing in oak casks and this gives the wine a very distinctive vanilla-like aroma. However, some producers are starting to cut the length of time the wine matures in the cask in favour of bottle-ageing.

The system of labelling can tell you something about how the wine has been aged. Vino de Crianza wine has had a minimum of twelve months in oak casks and will be at least three years old.

Reserva wines are selected wines from a good harvest and will have had at least thirty-six months between cask and bottle and will be at least four years old.

Gran Reserva wine is from an excellent harvest and will have had twenty-four months in cask and thirty-six months in bottle, or vice versa, and will be at least six years old.

These provisions apply to all Spanish wines.

Penedes wine producers, in contrast to Rioja, are experimenting with non-Spanish grape varieties, particularly Cabernet Sauvignon, and these are used both on their own and in blends. Some of the results have been first class. The wines are softer and fruitier than those of other areas, though the best ones do have good ageing capacity.

The *Navarra* area produces lighter wines with only a short period of ageing in oak barrels. They make very pleasant party wines.

Cleaning a barrel

WINE CONTAINERS

The vast majority of wines for sale in the shops and for export are sold in bottles. The standard size within the EEC is now 750ml or 75cl. Half bottles, litre and half litre bottles are also allowed.

Some wines are also sold in large sizes, as follows:

Chiantigianna	: 1⅓ bottles (Tuscany)	
Marie-Jeanne	: 1¾ bottles (Bordeaux and Coteaux du Layon)	
Magnum	: 2 bottles	
Double Magnum	: 2 bottles	
Jeroboam	: 6.6 bottles (Bordeaux)	
Imperial	: 8 bottles	

At the other end of the wine scale, some cheaper wines are sold in conveniently-sized cans and cardboard tetrapaks. Larger quantities are packed into bag-in-the-box cartons with a dispenser. These allow users to drink as little or as much wine as they want without having to worry about the remaining wine going off. But even with modern technology, the wine does not remain in peak condition for long.

STORING RED WINE

Some wines such as French Vins de Pays, Beau-jolais Nouveau and Valpolicella are designed for immediate drinking, but most red wines benefit from a while in store. This can vary from six months to a year for the better supermarket and off-licence chain wines, to five to ten years for fine wines bought from a specialist merchant.

Starting a cellar or stock of wine does not necessarily mean that you have to have a real cellar in the basement. Many other places will do just as well. The ideal wine store has a constant temperature, is dark but damp-free, and has good ventilation and no vibration. The most critical factor, however, is temperature. This should be between 10 and 15°C and, most importantly, there should be no sudden changes in the temperature.

The wine bottles should be stored on their sides. If the bottles are stored upright, the corks dry out and air gets into the bottles, spoiling the wine.

Do remember to keep some sort of list of the bottles you have, and where each one is stored if you are using several storage spaces.

VINTAGES

Unless the climate is constant, the quality of the wine produced in a region will vary from year to year. Set out below is a vintage charge for European wines, based on a scale of 0–7: 0 is poor and 7 is exceptional. These ratings give a general idea of the standard of wine produced in a given region and year, but individual wines may be much better or worse than the average. For a detailed assessment you need to know how the individual growers fared that year. Wines from outside Europe do not usually have such a big difference between vintages.

	France			Italy	
	Red Bordeaux	*Red Burgundy*	*Rhône*	*Tuscany*	*Piemonte*
1988	6	7	7	6	5
1987	4	6	5	4	6
1986	6	5	5	6	6
1985	6	6	6	7	7
1984	4	5	4	4	3
1983	6	6	6	7	6
1982	7	5	4	6	7
1981	6	4	5	4	5
1980	4	5	5	6	6
1979	6	5	6	6	6
1978	6	7	7	7	7
1977	4	4	3	6	3
1976	5	6	6	3	3
1975	6	3	6	6	3
1974	4	5	3	5	6
1973	4	4	4	3	4
1972	3	4	4	3	2
1971	6	6	5	7	7
1970	7	5	6	6	6

	Spain		Portugal		
	Rioja	*Penmedes*	*Dão*	*Barrada*	*Port (Vintage)*
1988	5	4	—	—	—
1987	5	7	—	—	—
1986	5	7	5	5	—
1985	6	5	7	7	6
1984	5	6	4	4	—
1983	5	5	7	7	6
1982	7	6	5	5	5
1981	6	4	4	4	—
1980	5	5	7	7	5
1979	5	4	4	4	—
1978	5	7	5	6	6
1977	3	5	4	4	7
1976	5	4	4	4	—
1975	5	6	6	7	4
1974	4	5	6	6	—
1973	5	6	4	4	—
1972	3	7	4	6	4
1971	3	5	6	4	—
1970	7	6	7	7	6

SERVING RED WINE

RED WINE AND FOOD

The traditional approach is to serve light red wines with white meat and poultry, fuller red wines with red meat and game, and heavier reds or port with cheese. These generalisations are quite useful, but there is no need to stick to them slavishly.

Choose a wine which is both to your taste and complementary to the food. If your favourite wine is a fragrant Beaujolais cru, such as Fleurie, serve it with a classic roast or grill rather than with a strong mustard sauce or a spicy casserole which would swamp it. The latter would stand up to a Rioja or a Portuguese Garrafeira.

The only way to find out what goes best with what is to experiment. After all, the classic Burgundian recipe for Oeufs en Meurette uses the local red wine as a medium for poached eggs, despite the fact that most experts suggest that eggs do not go with wine – and the dish is delicious!

Red wine and fish is another frowned-upon combination, and indeed if served with white fish some red wines do seem to take on a metallic taste. However, strongly flavoured oily fish does not seem to have the same effect, and both the Spanish and the French are quite happy to eat dishes such as Carp en Meurette and Eels in Red Wine. Salmon, too, can quite happily be served with red wine. Try a Sancerre rouge, a young and fruity Burgundy or even a Crozes-Hermitage from the Rhône.

Oriental food can be difficult to accompany, but young and fresh red wines, such as Beaujolais Nouveau and Valpolicella, are excellent. Beaujolais also goes well with spicy Thai food.

'Let's have wine and women, mirth and laughter
Sermons and soda water the day after.'

Don Juan, Lord Byron (1788–1824)

TEMPERATURE

Red wine should normally be served at room temperature, but this does not mean the temperature at which many people keep their centrally heated homes.

Ideally, full-bodied wines such as aged claret, Burgundy, Rioja and Barolo should be served at 15 to 17°C, and younger wines from those areas at 13 to 16°C. Very light wines such as Beaujolais, Valpolicella and red Sancerre may be served lightly chilled at around 10 to 11°C.

If the wine from your cellar is too cold the best way to heat it is to pop it quickly into a bucket of warm water. Placing the bottle on or by a heat source such as a radiator doesn't really work properly as it tends to heat, and indeed overheat, only part of the bottle.

'Dinner at the Huntercombes possessed only two dramatic features – the wine was a farce and the food a tragedy.'

A Dance to the Music of Time: The Acceptance World
Anthony Powell (1905–)

OPENING AND DECANTING WINE

A good corkscrew is the only really essential piece of equipment! Remember to remove the capsule that covers the top of the bottle as this is made of lead. Remove the cork, then wipe the mouth of the bottle with a clean cloth to remove any mould or dirt.

Very occasionally, the wine is corked. This does not refer to the fact that some of the cork has crumbled into the wine, but that the cork has been contaminated with a mould which gives off a very nasty smell.

Nowadays, port and aged claret are really the only wines which are likely to throw a sediment and so need decanting. Position a bright light, such as a candle, behind the shoulder of the bottle so that you can see when the sediment reaches the neck end, and pour the wine from the bottle into the decanter in one steady movement.

Wines change when they come into contact with air: younger wines for the better and older ones sometimes for the worse. Experts tend to disagree on how long a particular wine should be opened before it is drunk, but generally speaking the younger the wine, the more it will benefit from an hour or so in the air.

GLASSES

A good glass should have a stem long enough to give a comfortable grip and a wide enough foot to give a steady base. Do not fill the glass too full as space should be left to enjoy the bouquet. Tulip-shaped glasses and Paris goblets are fine for serving any kind of red wine. Traditional Burgundy glasses with a large bulb at the base and a wider rim are attractive for wines from the region, but take care not to over-fill as you will use up a bottle on the first round!

'By insisting on having your bottle pointing to the North when the cork is being drawn and calling the waiter Max, you may induce an impression on your guests which hours of laboured boasting may be powerless to achieve. For this purpose, however, the guests must be chosen as carefully as the wine.'

The Chaplet
Hector Hugh Munro Saki (1870–1916)

WINE RECIPES

CLARET CUP

This recipe is designed to brighten up a fairly ordinary bottle of red wine. Cheap own-label or clarets are ideal. You can vary the strength by the amount of soda water you add.

1 bottle ordinary claret
2 fl oz (50 ml) Grand Marnier or Cointreau
2 fl oz (50 ml) brandy
2 fl oz (50 ml) lemon juice
1 orange, sliced
1 lemon, sliced
1 red-skinned apple, sliced
1 teaspoon sugar (optional)
soda water

Place all the ingredients except the soda water in a large bowl or jug and chill in the fridge for 1 hour. Just before serving, add soda water to taste.

Makes 10 servings

RED WINE PUNCH

The original punch came from India where it was made with locally produced arrack. It became the custom to use five ingredients: spirits, tea, sugar, fruit juice and water. The Hindi word for five is *pantsch* and this soon became anglicised to 'punch'.

Nowadays, punch is made with all kinds of alcoholic drinks – in some cases the more, the merrier. However, in practice it is probably more sensible to stick to two or three drinks, let down with plenty of fruit juice or lemonade.

2 bottles red wine
1 bottle ruby port
1 miniature bottle brandy or fruit brandy
2 oz (50g) sugar
juice of 4 oranges
juice of 2 lemons
1 pint (600 ml) lemonade or soda water
ice cubes
sliced oranges, lemons and apples

Pour the wine, port and brandy into a punch bowl and stir in the sugar. Stir until all the sugar has dissolved. Add all the remaining ingredients and serve at once.

Makes 25 servings

SANGRIA

This was originally a very simple drink made by adding sugar and ice cubes to any kind of Spanish red wine. Today the recipes tend to be rather more elaborate. Here is one from a bar on the Costa Brava.

2 bottles Spanish red wine
2 tablespoons white sugar
1 miniature bottle Triple Sec or Cointreau
juice of 2 lemons
ice cubes
sliced oranges, lemons and apples

Pour the wine into a large jug or bowl and stir in the sugar. Continue stirring until all the sugar has dissolved. Next add the liqueur and the lemon juice and stir again. Add plenty of ice cubes (at least a trayful) and float the fruit on the top. Serve at once.

Makes 12 servings

WASHINGTON COOLER

This is a sparkling red wine cup devised in the States. Try it round the pool or in the garden in hot weather.

1 bottle robust red wine (Zinfandel or Côtes du Rhône)
½ bottle dark rum
1 pint (600 ml) orange juice
3 oz (75 g) sugar
1 litre chilled soda water
orange slices

Mix the wine, rum, orange juice and sugar in a bowl and stir until all the sugar has dissolved. Just before serving add the soda water. Garnish each glass with a slice of orange.

Makes 20 servings

'There was an old man whose remorse
Induced him to drink Caper Sauce
For they said, if mixed up with some cold claret cup
It will certainly soothe your remorse.'

Nonsense Verse
Edward Lear (1812–88)

Port Negus

Negus was the name given to certain types of punch invented by Colonel Francis Negus during the reign of Queen Anne. This one is typical of the times.

1 bottle ruby port
1 lemon, sliced
2 pints (1.2 litres) boiling water
1 miniature bottle brandy (optional)
sugar
grated nutmeg

Warm the port in a saucepan with the lemon. Just before it reaches boiling point add the water and remove from the heat. Add the brandy, if using, and sugar and nutmeg to taste. Serve in hot glasses.

Makes 18 servings

Spanish Bollan

1 bottle Spanish wine
3 oz (75 g) sugar
grated nutmeg
lemon slices

Heat the wine, sugar and nutmeg almost to boiling point, stirring until all the sugar has dissolved. Pour into warmed glasses and add a slice of lemon.

Makes 6 servings

MULLED WINE

There is nothing more welcoming than a glass of hot mulled wine on a cold winter's evening, but if you are planning to serve mulled wine at your next party it will pay to get organised.

Make the mulled wine in advance. Pour it into warmed bottles and keep it warm in a tub of hot water. The wine can be served from the bottle or transferred to a heated punch bowl. Remember to warm the glasses, too, or they may crack when you pour the hot wine into them. Another way of preventing the glasses from cracking is to place a teaspoon in them while you pour in the hot wine.

Mulled wine is basically a mix of hot wine with sugar and spices. Brandy, rum or a fortified wine such as port can be added for extra strength and slices of lemon give it a good flavour. Don't let the mixture boil or the alcohol will evaporate.

Never use your best wine for this party drink. You really will not taste the pleasure of it. An inexpensive red wine will do just fine. Most branded wines and some vins de table will probably be improved by the process!

Winter Warmer

4 bottles red wine
1 pint water
¼ bottle brandy or dark rum
1 stick cinnamon
3 cloves
1 lemon, sliced
pinch ground mixed spices (optional)

Pour the wine, water and brandy or rum into a large pan. Add the cinnamon stick. Push the cloves into the lemon slices and add with the mixed spices, if using. (If you want your mulled wine to remain absolutely clear, do not add the ground spices.) Heat the mixture to just below boiling and leave to stand for 30 minutes. Gently reheat, but do not allow the mixture to boil.

Makes 30 servings

'In vino veritas' – Truth comes out in wine

Natural History XIV, Pliny the Elder (AD 23–79)

GLUHWEIN

There are a number of forms of this popular German warmer. This is one of the simplest. However, you can buy special sachets of Gluhwein spices. These are added to the wine while it is heating.

2 bottles red wine
8 teaspoons brown sugar
ground cinnamon
8 slices of lemon

Pour the red wine into a saucepan and bring to just below the boil. Place a teaspoon of sugar, a dash of cinnamon and slice of lemon in each glass and top up with the hot wine.

Makes 8 servings

RED WINE TASTE GUIDE

A guide to red wine has been drawn up by the Wine Development Board in London. It uses a simple five-point alphabetical scale.

The guide is intended to help new or inexperienced wine-drinkers. It covers all kinds of red wine, but not those fine vintage wines which are intended to mature in the bottle.

The five categories identify red wine in terms of total taste or the impression they make upon the palette.

Starting at A, the wines are undemanding and very easy to drink. At E, at the other end of the scale, are the bigger and more concentrated styles with a greater sensation of depth and fullness.

The categories are identified on a special logo. These may be found on the supermarket or off-licence shelf, though they will not be found on the bottle.

A

Bardolino	German red wines
Beaujolais	Touraine
EEC table wines	Valdepenas

B

Beaujolais Villages and Crus	Red Burgundy
Chinon	Saumur
Côtes du Roussillon	Valencia
Merlot	Valpolicella
Navarre	Vin de Pays
Pinot Noir from all countries	

C

Bergerac	Corbières
Blended red from Australia, New Zealand, South Africa and Yugoslavia	Côtes du Rhône
	Minervois
	North Africa
Bordeaux Rouge/Claret	Rioja

D

Bairrada	Châteauneuf du Pape
Blended red from Hungary	Chianti
Cabernet Sauvignon from Australia, Bulgaria, California, Chile, New Zealand, Romania and South Africa	Dão
	Fitou
	Medoc
	Syrah

E

Barolo	Recioto
Crozes-Hermitage	Shiraz from Australia and South Africa
Cyprus red	
Greek red	

TASTING AND ASSESSING RED WINE

All you need to taste and assess wine are the senses of sight, smell and taste – plus a little practice.

COLOUR

The colour and appearance of the wine are the first pointers. The wine should be clear and bright. The actual colour and the amount of fading will tell you something about the grape varieties used and the age of the wine. For example, the Pinot Noir grape used for red Burgundy tends to give a fairly light colour, whereas Bordeaux wines have a deeper, more brick-like colour. The Gamay grape grown in the Beaujolais has a very purple colour when young. If you check the colour of the wine you buy, you will get to know these and other variations.

The colour of wine fades as it grows older. This fading shows first on the rim of the wine. The first faint hints of orange or brown are often an indication that the wine is reaching its prime.

SMELL

The smell, or bouquet, of a wine can also tell you a great deal about it. First of all, you can immediately tell if the wine is corked or has gone off in some way. Quite simply, it will smell horrible.

As with colour, certain grapes have quite distinctive aromas, and the more you smell different wines, the more you'll come to recognise the specific grape varieties. Young wines tend to smell more fruity than older ones, and wine which has been aged in oak casks gives off a wonderful vanilla smell.

Some very young or very cheap wines do not have much of a bouquet. It helps to rotate the wine in the glass as this agitates and acerates the wine and allows it to give off as much aroma as possible.

TASTE

The taste of the wine really confirms what your nose has told you, but taste will also help you determine how dry or sweet the wine is and its acidity and tannin levels. The latter has a harsh taste and produces a feeling of a coating on the tongue and teeth. Tannin is an essential element in a young wine which is expected to last, so if there is little or no tannin in the wine, drink it at once.

It is important to notice the flavour that is left in the mouth after swallowing the wine, and also how long this flavour lasts. Poor wine leaves little or no after-taste or finish. Good wines linger for a while.

TASTING TERMS

Here are a few of the terms which you might encounter in your merchant's wine descriptions.

Austere: Usually refers to an underdeveloped wine.

Baked: A 'hot', rather earthy smell, due to excessive sunshine.

Balance: The ratio between fruit, acidity, tannin and alcohol. These four should be in balanced harmony.

Body: The weight of the wine in the mouth.

Closed: A wine which does not smell or taste as much as you would expect.

Fruity: This refers to the flavour of the grapes, but is not necessarily grapey.

Oaky: A taste imparted to wines from ageing in oak casks.

Tough: A full-bodied wine with lots of tannin – probably a good wine for the future.

Bordeaux vineyard

HINTS AND TIPS FROM BELOW STAIRS

TO CLEAN A DECANTER

Cut some brown paper into very small pieces so that they will go into the neck of the decanter. Shred a little soap finely and add with tepid water. (Not hot water, which may crack the glass.) Add a little pearl of ash if the decanter is very dirty. Tie a small sponge on to a piece of cane and use it to work the mixture round the glass. Rinse the decanter with clean cold water. Turn it upside down and place it on a rack to dry.

A Footman's Guide (1840)
James Williams

TO PREVENT DECANTER STOPPERS STICKING

Wrap a piece of thin paper round each stopper before you put it away. If the stopper should at any time stick, breathe on it, or put one or two drops of sweet oil round the stopper, close to the mouth of the decanter, or just dip the neck into warm (not hot) water and it will soon loosen.

A Footman's Guide (1840)
James Williams

To Render Red Wine White

If a few quarts of well-skimmed milk be put to a hogshead of red wine, it will soon precipitate the greater part of the colour and leave the whole nearly white.

The Complete Servant (1825)
Samuel and Sarah Adams

To Detect Adulterated Wine

Heat equal parts of oyster shells and sulphur together and keep them on white heat for fifteen minutes and when cold mix them with an equal quantity of cream of tartar; put this mixture into a strong bottle with common water to boil for one hour and then decant into ounce phials and add 20 drops of muriatic acid to each; this liquor precipitates the least quantity of lead, copper, etc., from wines in a very sensible black precipitate.

The Complete Servant (1825)
Samuel and Sarah Adams

FOOD RECIPES

BOEUF BOURGUIGNONNE

The secret of this luxuriant Burgundian dish lies in the long, slow cooking and in the addition of a calf's foot, which gives a thick, velvety sauce.

1½ lb (700 g) topside or braising beef, trimmed and cubed
½ bottle red Burgundy
1 bouquet garni
16 button mushrooms, stalks reserved
4 oz (125 g) unsmoked streaky bacon, cut in one thick piece, if possible
1 large onion, peeled and sliced
1 calf's foot
salt and freshly ground black pepper
16 baby onions, peeled

Place the beef in a bowl with the red wine, bouquet garni and mushroom stalks and leave to stand for an hour or until required.

Preheat the oven to 300°F/150°C/Gas 2. Cut the bacon into small dice and fry in their own fat in a heavy-bottomed casserole. When the fat is running well, fry the button mushrooms all over and place on one side. Next fry the sliced onion until lightly browned. Remove the meat from the marinade and fry with the onions until well sealed. Add the calf's foot, the marinade and seasoning. Cover with a lid and bring to the boil. Transfer to the oven and cook for about 3 hours.

Remove the meat, calf's foot and bouquet garni from the cooking liquor and process the liquor in a blender, or rub through a sieve. Return to the casserole with the meat. Add the baby onions and the mushrooms and cook for a further hour.

Serves 4

'There was an old Man of Vesuvius
Who studied the works of Vitruvius
When the flames burnt his book, to drinking he took
That morbid Old Man of Vesuvius.'

Nonsense Verse, Edward Lear (1812–1888)

SAUERBRATEN

This German marinated pot roast of beef is traditionally served on high days and holidays. Dumplings and braised red cabbage are the usual accompaniments.

4 rashers lean bacon, cut into strips
4 lb (2 kg) topside or forequarter of beef, rolled
2 onions, sliced
1 carrot, sliced
2 stalks celery, trimmed and sliced
6 juniper berries, crushed
1 teaspoon salt
black pepper
2 bay leaves
1 pint (600 ml) red wine
½ pint (300 ml) white wine or vinegar
1 oz (25 g) dripping
4 oz (150 g) ginger cake, crumbled

Push the strips of bacon through the meat with a skewer and stand the meat in a deep dish. Place the onions, carrots, celery, juniper berries, seasoning, bay leaves, wine and vinegar, if used, in a pan and bring to the boil. Leave to cool and pour over the meat. The meat must be covered by the marinade: if there is not sufficient liquid, add a little more wine. Cover and leave to stand in the fridge for two to three days, turning from time to time.

Preheat the oven to 325°F/170°C/Gas 3. Drain the meat well, retaining the marinade. Fry the meat in the dripping until it is well sealed then place in a deep casserole dish. Pour on the marinade and cook in the oven for 3 hours. Remove the meat to a serving dish and keep hot.

Discard the bay leaves and purée the cooking liquor and vegetables in a blender. Pour into a pan and add sufficient ginger cake crumbs to give the sauce a fairly thick consistency. Heat through, beating with a wooden spoon, but do not allow to boil. Pour some of the sauce over the meat and serve the rest in a sauceboat.

Serves 8

The Cooper

'Who does not love wine, women and song
Remains a fool his whole life long.'

Attrib. Martin Luther (1483–1546)

Steak À La Bordelaise

Bordeaux cooks will tell you it is impossible to make an authentic Steak à la Bordelaise anywhere other than in Bordeaux – the reason being that you need to grill the steak over three different species of vine twigs!

6 shallots, peeled and finely chopped
4 oz (125 g) butter
1¼ pint (150 ml) beef stock
4 entrecote steaks
4 oz (125 g) cepes or other mushrooms, sliced
¼ pint (150 ml) red Bordeaux wine

Gently fry the shallots in half the butter for 2–3 minutes without browning. Add the stock and bring to the boil. Cook until the liquid has reduced by half.

Heat 1 oz (25 g) of the butter in a heavy frying pan until very hot and fry the steaks for 2–3 minutes on each side. When the steak is cooked to your liking, remove to a heated dish and keep warm. Quickly sauté the mushrooms in the pan juices and transfer to a warm plate.

Add the shallots, stock and red wine to the pan and bring to the boil. Boil rapidly to reduce the sauce – 3–4 minutes. Cut the remaining butter into small pieces and beat into the sauce. Add the mushrooms and pour over the meat. Serve at once.

Serves 4

Coq Au Vin

The thrifty French housewife used this recipe to tenderise tough old cockerels, and there are similar recipes from other parts of the world too. Use any kind of medium to full-bodied red wine.

1 × 4 lb (1¾ kg) chicken, with liver if available
salt and pepper
3 oz (75 g) butter
4 oz (125 g) thick cut streaky bacon, diced
12 button onions
1½ oz (30 g) plain flour
1 clove garlic, crushed
8 oz (225 g) button mushrooms
4 tablespoons brandy
1 bottle red wine
4 slices white bread, cubed
oil for frying

Cut the chicken into 8 pieces and season well, reserving the liver separately. Heat half the butter in a pan and fry the bacon and onions until well browned. Remove from the pan and keep on one side. Fry the chicken pieces in the same pan, adding a little more fat if necessary. When the chicken is browned, sprinkle on the flour and stir well. Add all the remaining ingredients except the liver, bread and oil, and bring to the boil. Cover and simmer for 45 minutes.

Cut the chicken liver, if available, into small pieces and fry in the remaining butter, until just cooked. Rub through a sieve with the cooking fat and keep for the sauce.

Fry the bread cubes in cooking oil until golden all over and keep on one side.

Remove the chicken, bacon and vegetables from the pan and keep warm in a serving dish. Strain the sauce into a clean pan. Add the puréed liver mixture and bring to the boil. If the sauce is too thin, boil to reduce a little. Pour the sauce over the chicken, sprinkle with the prepared croûtons and serve.

Serves 4–6

PRUNES IN RED WINE

Prunes are popular in southwest France where cooks marinate them in red wine before cooking.

8 oz (225 g) dried prunes, washed
1/2 pint (300 ml) Bergerac or light Cahors
grated rind and juice of 1 orange
*   or 3 tablespoons orange liqueur (optional)*

Place the prunes in a bowl and pour the wine over them, making sure that the prunes are completely covered. Leave to stand overnight in the fridge. Transfer the contents of the bowl to a saucepan and cook the prunes, either on their own or with the orange rind and juice or liqueur, for 10–15 minutes.

Serve hot or chilled.

Serves 4–6

CURES FOR HANGOVERS

Unfortunately for most of us, excessive consumption of wine leads to a hangover, and there are probably as many cures for the condition as there are sufferers.

Sensible cures include the use of vitamin C and the B complex. Alcohol tends to destroy these vitamins and so they will need to be replaced after drinking. Alcohol also causes the body to dehydrate and it makes sense to replace this water as soon as possible. Always try to drink at least as much water as you have drunk wine, and twice as much water as port.

More extravagant cures include proprietory drinks such as Underburg or Ferne Branca, or the notorious Prairie Oyster. The latter consists of a whole raw egg, carefully placed in a large cocktail glass. To this is added half a measure of brandy, one teaspoon of Worcester sauce, half a teaspoon each of vinegar and tomato ketchup and some seasoning. The whole lot should be poured into the mouth in one go. It should then be allowed to trickle down to stimulate a sluggish stomach. However, it may not be wise to eat raw eggs, and in general these cures seem to be based rather more on shock treatment than on coaxing your system back into shape.

WINE AND RELIGION

Dionysus or Bacchus is best known as the god of the vine and hence of wine. His ecstatic worship was characterised by heavy drinking, thrilling music and wild orgies. These extravagant rites were essentially foreign to the clear intelligence and sober temperament of the Greeks and they more probably originated among the tribes of Thrace, who were notoriously addicted to drunkenness.

However, levity was not the only reason for the heavy drinking. Worshippers believed that by drinking the juice of the grape they were partaking of the real body and blood of their god, and the rites were considered to be a solemn sacrament.

A similar idea, in a much more temperate form, has persisted to this day and plays an important part in the Christian church's Sacrament of Holy Communion.

'Mine eyes have seen the glory of the coming of the Lord
He is tramping out the vintage where the Grapes of Wrath are stored.'

Battle Hymn of the American Republic
Julia Ward Howe (1819–1910)

ACKNOWLEDGEMENTS

The author and publisher would like to thank the following organisations for their help with information and statistics.

The Wine Development Board,
Five King's House,
Kennet Wharf Lane,
Upper Thames Street,
London EC4V 3BH.

Send a stamped self-addressed envelope for leaflets on Mulled Wines, Summer Wines and Sparkling Wines.

The Wine and Spirit Association of Great Britain and Northern Ireland,
Five King's House,
Kennet Wharf Lane,
Upper Thames Street,
London EC4V 3BH.

Other Titles In The Series

The Little Green Avocado Book
The Little Garlic Book
The Little Pepper Book
The Little Nut Book
The Little Mushroom Book
The Little Rice Book
The Little Tea Book
The Little Coffee Book
The Little Chocolate Book
The Little Curry Book
The Little Mediterranean Food Book
The Little Exotic Vegetable Book
The Little Exotic Fruit Book
The Little Yoghurt Book
The Little Tofu Book
The Little Breakfast Book
The Little Egg Book
The Little Potato Book
The Little Spice Book
The Little Herb Book
The Little Sherry Book
The Little Whisky Book
The Little White Wine Book